T E T H E R

TETHER

Laurelyn Whitt

Seraphim
EDITIONS

The publisher gratefully acknowledges the financial assistance of the Canada Council for the Arts.

Canada Council   Conseil des arts
for the Arts   du Canada

Library and Archives Canada Cataloguing in Publication

Whitt, Laurelyn
        Tether / Laurelyn Whitt.

Poems.
ISBN 978-1-927079-13-3

        I. Title.

PS8645.H569T48 2013   C811'.6   C2013-901265-6

Editor: George Down
Cover Design and Typography: Rolf Busch
Cover Art - Julie Tremblay, Sculptor
            Reflections Series

Published in 2013 by
Seraphim Editions
54 Bay Street
Woodstock, ON
Canada N4S 3K9

Printed and bound in Canada

"That the things have us and that it is not we who have the things."

– Maurice Merleau-Ponty

CONTENTS

WELL WITHOUT END

A well neglected,
a woman warns me,
becomes so deep
it goes right through

past down into
up and on down
again, a Mobius

trick turning two
directions into one, or

grief, when it slips
from its lip of stone,
descending

shaft extending

into long liquid
silences it can
never leave
never reach.

Within you, a
continuum passes
through itself.

Words entering such
places drop like small
pebbles.

Listen.

There is nothing.

They are falling still.

CONFLUENCE NEAR PUGET SOUND

Four rivers flow
in tandem here:

the Hoko and the Sekiu, the Elwha
and the Clallam. The pull

of brine overcomes them,
    a longing to slip
    the lock of land, to merge with
    one another,
    dissolve into the sea.

I stand among them
    so still the gulls stretch
    their necks,
        cock a single eye at me

and forget the body
I am, how it hugs the earth;

    so still that words cannot
    find their way

    and lull me to sleep
    in the sweet silence
    of oceans.

The gulls, unblinking, pin me
to the world, to the Strait of
Juan de Fuca

this strip
    of sand.

Beyond, the huge, beating
heart of the Pacific breaks
and rises

    rushing toward me.

AFTERSHOCKS

Long ago in California, my dad
went out to sea. I stood,
hand inside my mother's. The ship
receded; the horizon
swallowed it up. The earth beneath
us did not move

           but waited. Then dishes
rattled in the cupboard; a vase fell
to the floor; my mother's hands
trembled. We huddled

under a table, my full five years
upturned. If the earth moves,
    I knew at once, a first certainty,
anything could happen. I dreamt

paws, claws to sink in shifting
ground, roots, long arms to pull the world
close, within me, to soothe the planet. By
rocking. Rocking

it back to
how it was. Or sinking
down, into deep stillness. As a breath

drawn in the wake of a vacuum, you
never take earth for granted after the first quake.

Years pass, lie jumbled among flowers
on my parents' graves. By the iris
is my 18th birthday; under the rose,
my 48th. And then, on the horizon, a ship

which only I see.
          It is fading.

The earth moves; a father leaves; anything can happen;
everything does.

SLIPPERS

Breaking trail after a twenty-hour snowfall, sinking to my knees in heavy powder with each step, the dogs dolphinning through drifts, burrowing their muzzles into faint exquisite scents, panting a wild joy through woods cloaked in the rapt silence only winter and storytellers evoke.

I follow, tracking aimlessly, down ravines, up hills, into a copse and out, trying to find what has left traces of itself behind, without any hint of why it wanders or where or whether it even is.

We return to the cabin not knowing. The dogs whimper, twitch and settle in to restless sleep, while I sit spent and disoriented by the wood stove, nodding, still tracking in dreams, touching the pile of clothes you left folded so neatly, holding bottles of medicine in my hands, reading a grocery list just begun – *grape juice*, you wrote, *crackers and syrup, treats for the dogs*. By your walker I notice your slippers. Like my boots and gloves by the door, they are warm now, waiting, open.

PRAYER

A whale surfaces and dives
   in the Strait of Juan de Fuca

    and the whole world goes up in praise.

In my palm a smooth white stone; in
   yours a swallow is cupped, wings

    splayed, fallen in the gap winds.

Untethered from thought and language
   a prayer relies on gesture, gratitude;

    a step into the simple, asking nothing.

A breath of air with the scent of sea;
   a memorial, holding what lives

    and once lived, together.

A LISTENING

"Ghosts are the language of the past, a 'kind of singing of things'." – A.S. Byatt

It could be sage's scent
on summer evenings,
or the delicate incense of
pine-filtered snow

or anything at all, inexorable
and fleeting; a thrush's

    waterfall of song, spilling,

    some sweet tremolo of leaves

    the vibrant quake
    of aspen,
          whatever it is

it sets his daughter
dancing.

The sea stirs.

Their hands touch.

No one notices how
the hum of the world
grows

or their eyes half-close,
in a listening.

RE-EMERGENCE

Seventeen years later the brood
returns, tunnels up.

Translucent husks cling to every
vertical surface,
           a sudden nocturnal pox.

With a soft crack, skin splits
down their backs; they reappear
as pale aliens

unrolling wings, bodies
blackened, eyes like
setting suns.

If you were here we might exclaim
sotto voce, at how they lumber
in laboured flight, their large

lugubrious bodies.

It's eerie, we would whisper
into precipitous silence

when the sound of several million
      male cicadas singing
            stops.

Turning then, I might ask
why they emerge *fortissimo*,
strident   then leave us

summer air inexplicably still?

Hard to know, you would answer:
maybe what coheres them

disappears.

TERMINUS

March, again.

He sleeps by her photograph   greets
   her each morning   whispers as
   birds flock the feeders

while an indeterminate light
   filters through blue spruce:

   could be dawn, could be dusk
   could be a storm pending.

Low in the canyon, snow melts
   receding into dank woods
   and leaf-drenched pools

   skins of ice fracturing;

the last cottonwood leaves
   hang   heavy in the slack
   of winter.

This may be the year her absence
   gives way and   grief eases
   ceases to shudder through him.

If so, he will only know it
   in another
   and another

with the clench and twist of loss
   in advance   in retreat

   a glacial recession:

the withdrawal measured by
   scour,
   grind,
   creep.

SMALL TALK, AT DI'S COUNTRY DINER

"What do you know worth tellin', Russ?" the waitress asks, pouring the old man a cup of coffee. "Well lemme see now." He pauses, looks out the window. Scratches at the stubble on his chin. "Not much, I guess," then offers this: "Had my drive sealed last week." Another pause. Another long look out the window. "Gets kinda lonely out there," he adds, voice faltering. "But I suppose you get used to it." The waitress comments on how it seems to her it's usually harder on the men. Russ nods his agreement. "Women, they make a place a home. They care for it, enjoy it. Men, they don't do that." He keeps looking out the window, eyes searching. Finishes his coffee and gets up to go. "You take care out there, Russ." "I'll do it," he says. Tugs at his suspenders, pulls on a cap, leaves.

SENTIPENSANTE

Felt thought, the fishermen
call it, thought become

membrane, tethered to touch.

It is how he finds his
silver-haired wife, lost

to the pulsing world. She
begins in his hands,

    dark eyes glowing.
    Returns, returns.

Remains. Caught
in a shimmering net

words filtered through skin,
the truth of the body. Then

    he knows only warmth,
    birdsong. The scent
    of earth, of sea   and it is

a crossing over, not the bridging
of a rift.

ECHOLOCATION

When sight fails and hearing
   dims, memory is what there is

     to live in; nothing that passes
        into it, passes out of existence.

The body's memories travel
   in waves, like sound.

Sent out, they come back
   to us, leaving traces in the
      world, echoes in the sea.

The time they take to return
   tells us where we are, where

we have been, and are heading;
   how far we are from the
      remembered.

BUNAHAN

When the last speaker of Boro
falls silent,
who will notice

the first-grown feather
of a bird's wing? (*gansuthi*)

or feel how far pretending
to love (*onsay)* is

from loving
for the last time? (*onsra*)

Quiet and uneasy, in an
unfamiliar place (*asusu*)

no one sees her, or listens;
there is less of her
than there was.

The last speaker feels
Boro's world fall apart,

knowledge unravels:
healing plants go
unseen; the bodies of animals

are unreadable.

With a last thought, *onguboy*
(to love it all, from the heart),

she leaves fragments
of the world she held in place.

We touch their husks,
about to speak and
about not to speak
(*bunhan, bunahan*);

awash in loss,
incomplete.

BEADS

When the first prayer failed,
  the monks tried again

    on a decade of fingers.

  Soon they lost track,
hands grew confused

    prayers drifted in the elements.

    To anchor prayer, they
    dropped small stones but

found their differences distracting.

  Laps filled with prayer were
      heavy, so the monks sat still.

  Then the stones became one,
and were strung on a chain:

    standardized, concrete, portable.

    A technology of prayer
    that would not be contained;

it moved with nations.

  When the monks rode
    with the Conquistadores

  rosaries hung from their waists.

They bound the hands of the
  living, necklaced the dying and

      in their deaths replaced them
    spreading like black wreaths

over empty pillows.

BLUE SWING

"If the names are lost, our knowledge dies as well."
– Johan Christian Fabricius, Danish naturalist

In the playground outside the window
bright slides and ladders rust,
child-abandoned.

Last summer, a woman in a black
niqab stood there; her son played.
She spoke to him, English, hesitant;
already fluent he chattered back.

So it begins, with the snap
of syntax: a sentence falls
apart, verbs

scatter to the ground, gaps
between the said and the unsaid
widen.

Without leaving Sweden, Linnaeus
did the same, writing the history
of botany over, in Latin

erasing the cures of the Quechua,
the knowledge of the Nahua.

It was a second baptism, in America

renaming immigrants as they
left the ship. *Rosaria* and *Giuseppe*
slipped into *Rose* and *Joe*

disappeared into cities.

A blue swing yaws in the breeze;
no one sees this. It is emptier now.

Frost seals every surface. A dog
runs by, as though someone calls.

THE WALMART OF LANGUAGES

"Language has always been the perfect tool of empire." – Antonio Nebrija

The great assimilator greets you
with a smiling face and promises
of prosperity

wants you to believe it is for you,
with you, of you; that it is not
what it is

something unaccountably other,
entering with an expansive air
consuming

communities, swallowing the
local up. This is the global gulp;
it refuses

to negotiate. It is empire, the
culture of control, the control
of culture.

But Walmart still sells what
the small stores sold. After
English,

what?

BRAND

Two maps, superimposed
on a table before me:

the underground railroad and
the trail of tears.

All along the Mississippi,
they intersect;

a grid of lines, leaving settlers
behind.

One sweeps north in flight
and escape, the other west
with removal, forced marches.

They press into the face
of America, like a brand.

No matter how mighty the Mississippi,
the weight of this history
displaces its waters.

Along its banks, if you pause
long enough early enough

you hear voices, Indians
and bondsmen, whisper in the
cottonwoods, drifting with seeds.

This is how history and the river
came to be haunted.

WHEN THE MISSISSIPPI RAN BACKWARDS

*"For Tecumseh, the earthquakes were a signal that the Great
Spirit had finally taken a decisive hand in the affairs of his
people."* – J. Penick

The signs were thick
that winter;

rivers teemed
with the small bodies
of squirrels

gathered by the thousands
into deep and sober
phalanxes

pouring south
in great grey waves

that broke, unrelenting
on the broad Ohio.

Overhead the terrible
comet tore

a brilliant growing rip
in the sky.

A flaming arrow that
streaked southwest;

the forests glowed
day and night.

And like some bright
planet, Tecumseh came

to the Choctaw, Creek
and Chickasaw.

Soon, he said,
the earth will
swallow villages

and drink up the Mississippi.

TECUMSEH'S RETURN: THE QUAKES OF 1811-1812

When I return to Detroit, Tecumseh said,
I will stamp the ground. You will know
the Great Spirit has sent me.

The land became fluid, an inland sea
that rose and fell in massive furrows.
Forests crested on rolling swells, then
snapped like stems.

A violent tempest where there was no wind.
Shrill whistling, a constant hiss. And from
deep within the rocking earth, stabs of lightning
broke on thunder.

Dark clouds dropped over the astonished
faces of settlers. Their legs sank in a black
ooze. The smell of sulphur hung in the air
and Tecumseh was in Detroit:

Where today are the Pequot? the Narragansett?
the Mohican? Shall we let ourselves be destroyed in turn?
Geese screamed. Dogs howled. Fissures split
the ground. They gaped, northeast to southwest,

as though severing settler lands from the continent.

Whirlpools churned the rivers. Sunken logs shot
into the air. The Mississippi heaved, writhing
in her bed. Then into villages of the southern
tribes, ancient enemies poured. They streamed,

fearless, from the forest. Wolf, panther, bear
and fox mingled with deer, squirrel and rabbit.
With them came flocks of birds, that blanketed
the heads and shoulders of the people.

An uncommon alliance, they gathered
at the fires, the vision of Tecumseh come
true: a confederation of beings, united
by a ruptured world.

BRINCO

They are building a wall
down south, across the
Sonoran desert.

Several walls, impenetrable layers:

the first of metal, fifteen feet,
the second, eleven, of barbed wire.

And in between, a no-brown-man's-land
nine hundred feet of security

a zone to keep illegals home,
to sort the documented
from the un,

to hold the hordes at bay.

Not even lizards
will get through
to the north;

the southern desert will be
cut-off, isolated.

But when winds blow
sands shift, eroding;

birds alight between barbs
on the wire;

and bullets pass
through ghosts, dancing.

PENANCE

Assunta took the boat from Palermo alone, two small children in hand
to meet a husband three years gone, a cobbler without tools. It was 1916.
The country, deep in nativism, recorded her as Sicilian – lowest
of the low – noted the colour of her skin and renamed her children.
The entry officer being Irish – former lowest of the low – her little girl,
Rosaria, would be Rosalie and Pasquale, her son, became Pat.

The fishing village of Sicily faded into an immigrant ghetto in New
York. Urban poverty replacing rural. But without relatives nearby they
were poorer than before and without a patch for a garden, hungrier.
So when within a year of her arrival Assunta learned another child
was on the way she considered her barely surviving family. And,
with a reluctance that spilled into resignation, let herself think
the unthinkable act. Ending a pregnancy (the closest she could come
to naming it) was a mortal sin unlike any other. For it condemned an
innocent being forever to Limbo, an undefined state of perpetual
separation that hung somewhere between heaven and hell.

Assunta went through with it in a dark, dirty room then spent the rest
of her life in penance. Unable to speak of what she had done, unable
above all to confess it, she knelt day after day all day in churches,
holding who knows what kind of conversations with her God.
While at night, in the dark at home, she wore five layers of clothes
and sat rocking, rocking.

"She had no choice," explained Pat and Rose to the priest,
much later as Assunta lay dying. "Please just give her absolution."
But the young priest would not, insisting he must hear the words,
that Assunta must bring herself to say them. That until
and unless she did, he would not relieve her guilt, would not
offer absolution.

Assunta passed her last sixty years in a futile limbo of penance.
Knowing nothing could help, could be enough, that none of it would
matter. A lifetime later, the Church whose teachings she never
questioned revised its eight-hundred-year-old doctrine. Officially
banishing that eternal resting place which was, they declared, at odds with
"the greater theological awareness today that God is merciful".

Too late for Assunta, who died rosary in hand, still mourning
for another being. Trapped indefinitely in that suspended realm.
Knowing neither relief nor closure. Apologizing.

TRIPPING

"I was in prison for three years before I realized this could be done – throwing your mind somewhere else."
 – Death Row prisoner

He walks in the night. The path exact:
            (Five paces and turn.)
door, to bed, and back. The familiar rhythm
            (pace, turn)
within him. He focuses. Intently.
            (Five paces)
On sanity. Control. Separate the mind,
            (turning, pacing)
leave the body behind. Put it elsewhere
            (Five paces and turn.)
then go there, and stay. No one will know
            (turns, paces)
you're away. Or that it's happening:
            (paces and …

concrete and steel waver, blur,
   give way to late October. Scent

of damp pines, woodsmoke; hiss
   of coffee boiling over; Sam's

low tuneless whistle. Hands
   to the fire, Joe watches Orion

stalk. The chill night closes in. Half-
   smiles on stubbled faces, they

wonder about the elk this morning
   in the meadow; the trophy bull

       they just missed.

The monitors   in Control Central   line the wall.   I see everything.
That guy in D Block   Number 925   has been pacing for seven
hours.   He settles into it every night   him and some others.
Mostly those with serious time   start shuffling.   Like rats
in a cage   but with that weird mechanical precision.   Hard to say
why.   Exercise maybe   or boredom.   Maybe nerves in 925's case.
Three months ago   he gave up his appeals.   Now he's just waiting
for his date   with the needle.

GRASS

"The next journey has got to be better ... I got to figure in the next one I'm going to have a chance to do a little bit of good ..." – Joe Parsons

He was one of the good guys on death row, they agreed. Pretty classy. Even with the guards, one inmate said, going out of his way to be nice so they won't feel so bad about doing it. Mr. Joe, they called him. Out of respect. But with only 70 days of freedom between 18 and 35, he'd simply grown tired. Of boredom, the waiting, the inconsistencies.

You're constantly walking on thin ice, he sighed, trying to find the cracks so you don't fall through. What's okay one day isn't the next. They give you something then take it back, no explanations. Like when they started this new death row programming and let me out to wash walls. They put me with another guy, Cody. It was my first real contact in eleven years. We shook hands first thing, then patted each other on the back. I finally felt some human companionship. Less like a caged animal. Damn near a person. Then last month, they just stopped it. Why? Why are they doing this? What is the reason? The mind games, that's the reason I'm going. I'm tired of them. That wasn't the catalyst. Not even the final straw. Just another one. I've run out of energy, and stopped my appeals. Started to give things away. A pair of grey sweatpants (without the cord). A Star Trek T-shirt (the Next Generation). I'm happy to finally be going. I'm almost done. Dying is easy. It takes more courage to go on, to keep plodding along. Wouldn't it be easier, on the streets, for a woman to die rather than go on living with a man who beats her? I'm not talking about people with money. I'm talking about people like waitresses and janitors who only make enough to make ends meet and who have to keep on doing the same things over and over every day. The easy way would be to take a handful of pills; the suicide rate is not as high as it should be. We don't give enough credit for the survival instinct, or the guts to keep going. Me, I'm done with guts. What's going to happen won't exactly be suicide. I'm not the one who'll press the button. They're going to be putting the drugs into my system. Maybe that makes it a little easier, because I might hesitate.

Everybody on the block was thinking about him. Trying not to. *They'll take him at 10 o'clock today,* Cody said. *He's ready to go. He wants to go. But I'm not going to like it. This is the first execution since I've been in here. He's doing much better than anyone else. He's in there laughing and joking. That's what's helping me out. I honestly think most of his happiness is for those around him. When they're strapping him to the gurney I'll have my own farewell for him. I'll set out some chili with rice (I don't normally do this), and a root beer (and I don't drink root beer). Then at the stroke of midnight I'm going to salute him and eat it. Sounds weird, I know, but what else can I do?*

The warden meanwhile was ordering the lockdown, the drugs they would administer. Establishing the tie-down team, the clean-up team, security. They gave him a contact visit with his brother and a TV with a VCR for some movies. *There's a few I'd like to check out before I go*, he'd said. *I'm a big sci-fi fan. But they're not going to let me play basketball. They said it's kind of a political thing. Sooner or later the public will know, and see them being too nice to me.* But his first last wish was to walk on grass again, and when they moved him from death row to death watch, Mr. Joe had his chance. Took off his shoes. Felt the cool blades pressing up to his feet. And, he could swear it, the earth turning, turning beneath them.

THE AFTERLIFE OF JOSEPH PAUL

Envision the inverse of the Panopticon;
the Centre's all-seeing eyes displaced,
    lining the Periphery

    not gazing out at bodies in cells but in
        at the cells of bodies.

After the State executed Joseph Paul, they would not let his brother
touch him. The corpse, still warm, was transferred. *I don't condone
execution,* one scientist said, *but don't believe in wasting resources either.*
So Joseph Paul's body was preserved, frozen in blue gelatin.

What's become of our son? His parents, never consulted, persisted.
Starting at the feet (they were not told), *he was sliced into slides;
we shaved his body upwards. It took nine months to plane him away,
to conceive him as anatomical Adam. If he had a soul* (they didn't add
but might have), *we assure you we never found it.*

    Whoever said death is the ultimate release
    from belonging, never imagined the afterlife
        of Joseph Paul.

    Interred in virtual reality, all body and no body
    he flickers in intimate, endless detail; chilled
        in the blues

    of cyberspace, the singular Site of all sight.

KITE FESTIVAL

News item: seven people die in Pakistan.

Coloured sails ripple the sky.

They rise and plummet;
execute an aerial dressage

of controlled lunges, sharp
pivots.   Invisible hands

tether them, send signals.

Then grace and
art go dark; taut

wings, that cupped
and cut the wind,

fall slack, falter.

One by one, they descend
in inert loops, aimless

spirals; eddy and
drift to earth.

To those who declare the last
aloft, victor.   It soars;

string laced in glass
glinting in the sun,

and severs whatever it
touches or entangles.

Including the throat of
four-year-old Shayan,

who sat on his father's bike.

Head turned to the sky in
wonder, in awe   he collapsed,

dying in the arms that held him.

ANIMAL MEMORY

A dog
black, lop-eared and wary

fills the shelter with her waiting.

Someone enters one day,
or does not;   looks deep

into shadows, or away.

The bruised body trembles;
hesitant, a tail thumps;

eyes haunt impossible futures.

When the door shuts
it is much too late;

longing spills from the cage

pours through cracked windows
down the streets, among us.

Without expectations.

SOMETHING WONDERFUL

Waste rock, down a mountainside
where ore veins were stripped;
the remains huddle in mounds

tailing into streams; earth to
earth, leaching heavy metals.
Dark, lichen-encrusted, the slope

still breathes; decades tick and
small mammals hide; birds alight,
peck at scurrying insects.

The slope breathes; softly
exhales and inhales ghosts
caught when stopes collapsed

when air ran out, lungs
filling with strange gases
minds spilling into shafts

of light, then breaking
in caves as black and implacable
as pitch. The town waits,

folding in on itself; the weathered
boards of fences, homes
sag and settle into weeds; cars

rust patiently beside them. And
each morning, the steel greys
of dawn rise on it all. Expectant.

As though something wonderful
was about to happen, to the
breathing slope, the dogged town.

A VANISHING

"They live forever by not living at all."
– Aldo Leopold

So thick, the only sound was a
single massive wingbeat,
muting the air;

the nests bent and broke
the hardwoods.

Did they feel it in their bones,
a raptor circling

dropping its net of shadow
upon them like a stone?

On they came, endlessly on,
stretched in tiers, darkening
the skies for days. So thick

one shot brought down thirty or
forty bodies, plummeting to earth

by the thousands, the millions,

the death spiral moved
like a funnel cloud over the land.

Until it reached Martha

the last of her species,
dying in a zoo in Cincinnati;

her loneliness so great
it never left us.

THYLACINE

Staring warily from Tasmanian
bush, the tiger:
    embedded in a steel cage.

Her striped body merges
with bars, steps out of
    photographic stills

leaves tracks still
with us; a shadow that
    slips time

the exact moment
when extant becomes
    extinct.

Until we can prove
her absence, memory is
    maintenance ritual

links predator and prey together
like rock art;

    makes them implicit.

PICTOGRAPH: NINE MILE CANYON

He seems as stunned as I to have
made it through the centuries.

A tall slim figure from the Fremont
raises his left hand in greeting;

between us, more than a millennium.

Red dye stains his forearms; on mine,
sweat-streaked canyon dust. At either

end of a continuum of worlds,
we are speechless.

What is there to say?
Should we break into ontology?

Complain about the drought?
Debate the prospects of anticlimax?

Our failure to speak is,
in the scheme of things, a small one,

so long as this opening between
worlds   remains.

DELIQUESCENCE IN THE ATACAMA

The driest place on the planet
drier than the Negev,
than the Antarctic Dry Valleys

is a Chilean desert where
once in a decade it rains.

Even so, in the hyperarid core
of the Atacama, in the dry
halite rocks of the Salar

life happens, rarely.

On the cusp of dawn,
when the air is coldest

salt rocks suck in moisture
and microbes deliquesce.

They metabolize in the sunrise,
synthesize light;

on a good morning
they may even divide

before lapsing, hours later,
into dormancy.

Their brief bloomings
skirt the limits of life,
the limits of endurance:

deliquescence, then acquiescence
then back.

THE MUSIC WE CANNOT HEAR

Below middle C, fifty-seven octaves down
   lies a B-flat so deep it cannot

      be fathomed. The hum of the Perseus
   black hole rumbles from the halo of energy

surrounding it, rippling

   on the dark pond of the universe.
      Every ten million years its sound wave

   rises, joining others, each singing different
tones from dense centres. While we lean out

   from a moment of earth, immersed.

CAIRN-KEEPER

First a single stone
white, pear-shaped

resting on a slate-grey slab
in a clearing.

Then more, many
varying in size, in colour
and shape, in stability;

a grove of cairns
huddles the ground,
flanked by pine and cedar.

Stillness becomes shape,
density; a presence,
moves out
from within. Palpable:

the hush of pine needles
as they fall to earth,

of wind that shifts in the cedars.

Here is hallowed ground;
approach gently.

In such places, on such days
listening is all that is possible.

Waves of mist lift and
settle over the stones

eoliths of memory;
relinquished but alive
given up, given over.

They do not cover or contain;
they are composed.
I stand in a grove,

listening to cairns

being listened to.

WAR STORY

An old vet asked about his time in the war shifts his eyes to the nearest window. His voice quavers, a hand raises, halfway up halfway down, as though reaching for something or about to salute, as though to wave hello or goodbye or both. It begins to shake; he gazes far and away, down time, down space, down memory. When they find him – the images, the sounds, the smells – they grip his body in tremors, aftershocks: "It was hard," he says, "so very hard. We went through so much. No one knows." He has begun to cry, as have I; he because he knows and remembers; I because he does and cannot tell.

SAFE PASSAGE

There are beings who go between worlds.
They live before wind, hurtling elements.

Haunting the bows of boats. To watch over
sailors, you told me. On your arms, tattoos
of blue. Bottlenose dolphins.

I sat listening to stories of thrashing seas, of
submarines and submariners. Of my father.
Who rose and dove in the roiling Pacific.

A poet once, my favourite tale began, was
thrown into such waters; he lay drowning.
But his final words were so sweet or strong,

that dolphins came, cradling him to shore.

Nurses come and go now.   Shift your body
on the bed.   Your hand in mine, these long
evenings   as I search for songs   to lure

such beings.   Songs to go between worlds.

I would find one. I would sing it.

So dolphins will come, rising
below you.

AFTER

Some moor themselves with
friendships; others anchor offshore
distant, and alone.

WITHIN, WITHOUT

An infusion of elements: mist

the breath of water, pillowing
up the Sheepscot.   Thickening.

Dampening sound.

Even words, when they
reach the ear, congeal

lie limp in dark wet phrases

as chill and desolate
as a buoy, unseen

    clanging erratically

with the swell, lapse and
tug of the sea.

I want to grieve forever

you write, from the high
dry deserts of Utah, the sage
and mountain west:

without it who would I be?

Sealed in these salt fogs
on an estuary, I try
to answer
    tell you

       speak.

MAN WITH LIGHT IN HIS FINGERS

– after a painting by Sky Patterson

Someone poured you into this world
from another, the one
you are returning to.

A pitcher upended, into a velvet black pool;

if shadows have an essence, it is you.

It may be regret, or reluctance,
it may be reflex
at the radiance ahead

but you linger in your leaving,
shoulders turning:

"I have light in my fingers"
you whisper, *"My hands are confused."*

You could be any of us –
fingertips dipped in colours
so bright and vital they are

points of sublimation,
where the world enters veins
changes state.

We slip into and out of
your supple contours

feel the afterglow in our hands
and stretch them wide,

leaving behind
fragile handprints

on this side of a long
blank space.

AMBER

Within the stone that burns and floats
in the sea, inclusions:

> from an oak as old as the Cretaceous
> > three tiny flowers return

> from a web woven among dinosaurs
> > a piece of silk.

Stories paused and held, unfold, epochs later:

> a praying mantis attacked by ants,
> > keeps struggling

> mites, on the backs of bees,
> > hitchhike to the future

> and two spiders, locked
> > together, continue to mate

oblivious
to the ooze that overcame them
or seduced by something

viscous
a golden glow,

the piney scent of resin.

RECLAMATION

Into the liminal, my mother comes,
space of dream

of soft thunder: mourning doves
fill the room.

It is time, she says. My father
follows, becomes

    the chill of mountain air

    a fire, at dawn, smouldering

    ash and bones that sift to earth,
    returning to water

dissolving into seas, into
white beaches

    where I lean forward

    hands cupped, frantic
    with tenderness, at

    the swell
    the surge and break
    of his life.

DAUGHTERS

In the distance, a middle-aged
woman and her much older father;

he leans on a cane; she tucks
her arm through his.

They are silent together, walking.

At the next table is another,
with her mother.

Their heads are close,
grey and not-grey;
laughing.

Small, quiet intimacies,
once mine.

Everywhere I go,
they are. And everywhere,
they are not mine.

TOMBOY

Carriages are for dolls. Your
beautiful dolls. Only for dolls.
Remember.

But I was not my mother's
daughter. Carriages
were for rocks. For
moving dirt

    or if conditions permitted,
    mud and water.

Despairing of my domestic potential
at six, mother tried again at
twelve
    with a sewing box.

Scissors are for sewing, for
dresses and skirts. They are
not to be used otherwise.

But otherwise was all there was:
her child wore pants, cut leather

made saddles for horse statues,
pouches for stones, cradleboards
out of old snowshoes.

It is all there still is:

grown now, the child sits,
sewing box on lap

removes the scissors   then
hesitates

before trimming silk flowers.

In that pause all that falls
between mothers and daughters
enters.

The scissors are heavy, in my hands.
I turn them, turn them.

MOVING HANDS

The woman in the bed next to me
has no family,
    and very little time.

Hearing this, I become
a daughter
    keeping vigil through the night.

Eyes closed, she never wakes

but her hands I think could be
Scheherazade's, pantomiming
tale after tale

making, unmaking, remaking
worlds.

I memorize their slow dance
    absolving the living

    permitting them to let go

    her world turning away.

STRING FIGURES

Begin with a loop of
string, of words, a story;

let it circle quietly
in the blossom of hands.

Listen while an old voice
murmurs to a young one:

telling, untelling
retelling itself

netting space.
Wait

while those dying
linger; their fingers

weave an unendable
dance,

linking generations.
Filaments extend

sentences loop
into forms;

the past is strung
from present and future.

Hang them upon the heart.
Small containers

sieves of memory: what
children are left with

when parents leave them.

LEAVE-TAKING

Two figures swim,
   side by side, to where an
   estuary joins the sea;

a point of convergence.
   They grow smaller. Steeled
   blues of water and sky

wash into one another
   as they go, stroking,
   stroking with the tide.

Past the lobster pots and docks,
past the clanging buoy bell,
past the island with its lighthouse

   into the open ocean.

Much later, I wonder if
   I can just barely see them
   stroking long

   past the edges of the Atlantic,
   well beyond.

LIMBER PINE: CROWSNEST PASS

Bonsai'd by the elements. Rock-bound roots wound
around root-bound rocks. Stumpy

trunk capped by
balding crown. All bark
and little needle.

            Knotty and naked
at the throat of the Pass,
         your ragged signature scrawled
from foothills to sky

is underscored
by one bony limb, chinooked
to a long thin finger.

Your kin, the bristlecone, older by millennia,
hold out for the tree line. But you descend
         to stand among us. Hanging on.

Like the Kootenay. And the Blackfoot.
The miners who came after.

Part sentinel, part omen,
you drew them into the Pass. We follow,

arrested by serenity,
the sere caricature:

dead now, yet upright. Intent.

SONG FOR THE MINER'S CANARY

Working bird. Genus
Serinus.

They carried you down
fragile as fireflies in fruit jars

the black metal box,
a mine within a mine

heavy and dented, a cylinder
of oxygen on top.

You peered out through a bit
of screen,

a sun drop,
bright bolt
        singing.

    The shorter your claws
        the longer their lives
        so they pared them.

Did the bats cower
at your brilliance?

        Or hang
in envy at canorous
sound, silver slivers
transposing, up and down?

If you had a sad song
would you have sung it?

The miners whistled soft
encouragement,
        you poured music back

sending light and
        space and breath to coal-
        dusted hearts

until
thick quiet fell

as you swayed to sinuous gas,
claws gripping, slipping
the perch.

When you faltered and dropped they
sealed your box, pumped in air
       then grabbed you
       and ran.

Brought you home to serenade the family.

Working bird.
Genus Serinus.
       The glow within the tunnels.

Redundant now, displaced.

The stopes darker, less tolerable
       for having held you.

TURTLE MOUNTAIN, MOVING

i. *Deformation*

The Blackfoot skirted its shadows:

an unstable being, the mountain that
walks, limestone layered

over clastics and coal, its back
arched, a steep shell that crept
over eons, eroded

      by valley glaciers, the river
coursing at its feet, then companies
that drove in stakes, giant stopes

with forty foot pillars and vertical
shafts, to drain coal
      from deep thick veins.

At the summit fissures spidered, opened
to meet them. Meltwater trickled then
froze. Split the mountain apart.

No one paused to ponder the geomechanics
of failure, oblivious as stresses
mounted, reached their limits, pressed

past, into the brittle heart of unbending
rock.   Until fracture.   Rift.

There was a massive crack, the miners said,
a rumbling that rose and dove through thought,
pinning them beneath it. When the ground pitched

they rode it like a deck into the swell of an ocean.
Timbers breaking. The whinnies of horses billowed
in the tunnels. The mountainside sheared away,

      dissolving over them.

ii. Flow

Waves of sound spread,
regenerated,

vibrated rock-to-rock,
slide mass slipping and
pouring like water down
into the valley, across
it, then up, the dozing town
buried in an instant, dust
misting, the grey sea
of debris
       in frozen undulation,

Hokusai's Great Wave released

then returned to stasis,
to potency
       to wait.

AFTER THE TRAIN

The trains in our head pause politely
at the edge of memory, whisper

to be let in. They limn the horizon
with whistles and smoke.

This one is different.
It blasts right through.
Battering eyes, ears,
consciousness. Boring into.
The antithesis of poetry, it
clangs and asserts:
        I am coming, I am coming, I am coming.
Steel wheels slamming, clammering
rhythmically. An urgent crescendo
invades our dreams. Plunges
into sleeping streets, howling with need:
        through, through, through.
Scrawled with warnings, hauling our
worst nightmares, its black tankers breathe
in the windows. *Ammonia*, they hiss. *Molten*
        sulphur. Sulphuric acid and radioactive
        waste.
What we want most not to hear is the
screech of metal. The squeal of
momentum   checked.
The clang of cars bunching, jumping
the track.   Derailment.

Such trains change everything.

Like field mice in the path of an owl,
we fold up, inward. Draw skin taut

around bones. Retreat with the thought
of denouement.

Its wings flap, wild in our skulls.

THE MEDICINE LINE: Incision

To map is to metaphor, to let
two dimensions be

three and take on the world.

Take the arc that fell from the sky in the
nineteenth century

the one drawn from stars and sun

that pencil-thin curve
of the 49th parallel.

Let us suppose, its creators agreed,

that what is
not, is.

Let us see what a difference that makes.

So they spun a line, strung it
on mountains, sunk it in lakes

pressed it on prairies and forests.

A line that, as they imagined it,
was used

and as it was used became real.

A metaphor that slipped its leash.

A map that passed from make- to
made-belief.

And after the line, came the multitudes.

THE MEDICINE LINE: Geodesy

The earth dividers, with their exquisite tools: assorted transits
and theodolites   compasses and sextants   innumerable charts and
books   some carefully synchronized chronometers   great zenith
telescopes.   Come to practise the surveyor's art   come to cleave
the continent.

> *"the laws of both countries*
> *begin and end at that line"*

At first, anything served as markers. Iron pillar pyramids made in
Detroit. Stones piled in eight-foot cairns. Mounds of earth, hunkered
three miles apart.

Imposing order on the inchoate border. An ocean of prairie that
undulated, roiling with dust   a tangle of trees   green limbs
locked, intertwining   thrust and jumble of mountains   the suck,
the musk, the muck of swamp.

Latitude 49 degrees North: standardized, fixed. The boundary vista
cleared. The division visible. A string of small white obelisks studs
the land   through forests and bush, a twenty-foot swath   sustained
by herbicides, chainsaws.   If you stand in the middle they say
you can see the curve of the planet.

> *"people need to know that when*
> *they step across that line they're*
> *stepping into a foreign country"*

Only on the lakes were they stymied. There, where the line dissolves,
disappears. Where stories of empire intermingle.

THE MEDICINE LINE: The Other Side

"the last political symbol of hope for the
nineteenth-century plains native" – Beth LaDow

Perhaps one side was more adamant
than the other, and
    little more than this.

But the Great White Father's
glinting ultimatum
    reservation or extermination

hung like a sabre, fell
across the south

as the Great White Mother
    ambivalent, mumbled

from both sides of her mouth.

And hearing them, the choice
was plain.   Sanctuary.

Sitting Bull would make it,
Chief Joseph did not.

Riding for that gap in the world.

Riding where the Long Knives stopped.

Their lathered horses, racing north
    raised a dark fog of dust

    manes streaming
    muzzles reaching

for a place of such power
that no law crossed.

    The line was sacred, they said.

Back then, if you made it to the border
things were
different.

THE MEDICINE LINE: Border Dream

"We are segregated by a line. It has taken away our relationship." – Peter Strikes With a Gun

Somewhere between the Sweetgrass and Cypress Hills,
fence wire hums with
the failure of borders

hawks soar, dryland
sparrows dart and dip.

Over a charged strip of
land, the newcomers'
knife-trick

flayed earth

Blue Flax is growing, and
Prairie Smoke.

Bison cross in black clouds,
the great horse cultures
converge

to make treaty,
shed the robes
of state.

Dry, rain shadow winds sweep the grasslands of the high
northern plains. Comb
the 49th parallel.

On a hot day, in
Palliser's Triangle

there is a mirage-like
presence: obelisks

blur, shift shape,
location and nature

float above the earth.

THE MEDICINE LINE: Border Fatigue

The constant creep of the continent
as it goes on covering itself

obscuring borders with
rock slides and undergrowth

water shift of river banks,
wind shift of dunes.

Bison rubbed against the original
markers, skewing them. Stone

cairns collapsed and spread. Now
obelisks tilt at crazy

angles, sinking headstones
that have just given up or given in.

Barbed wire fences sag
and mysteriously disappear.

Who knows what comes of them?

Some claim herds of wild barbed wire
horses have been seen in the foothills

ridden by barbed wire Indians, pursuing
barbed wire bison

with barbed wire missionaries and treaty
commissioners pursuing the lot.

Hallucinations, probably
another symptom of border fatigue.

All of it muddles the effort
to hold the Parallel in place,

frustrates its Keepers, who grasp
256 official boundary maps

in one hand, and 20-odd treaties
conventions and agreements in the other

muttering about how hard it is
to hold the line, how border

maintenance never ends
and who can afford it?

Conspiracy theories of nature
multiply: what states define

the land undermines. Fifty-three
percent of those polled believe this.

Who could doubt it?

CHINOOKED

Not itself on the other side.
Hard to recognize.

Something furry, wet and chill
rises from the Pacific.

Shakes itself dry. Climbs to the
spine of the Rockies then

    shifts shape, slips leeward
    towards us.

The atmosphere alters; we sniff
the air, as though stealth had a scent

we could identify, and the pounce
was nearly upon us.

At the ridgeline, standing wave
clouds form; eerie lenticular lenses

obscure the peaks. Stationary
saucers where the Snow Eater sleeps

before it howls down to meet us.

Melting ice with its desert thirst, a
hot dry breath scours the Pass, wailing

another mid-winter Overture to Spring
in the rain shadow of mountains.

Part respite, part titillation.

Teased from dormancy we bow
to the horizon, one being: aspens,

limber pines, people. Leaning
forward, leaning away. Diagonals

of enduring. Seared by streams
of leaves, of loess. Purged by litter,

coal dust. Senses and sense
in conflict, chinooked
believing both,

believing neither.

FIVE UNKNOWN SCHOOLGIRLS AT ST. MARY'S

*"I can look into their eyes and their spirit
lives through them."* – Mi'ksskimm

Missing from the image
is what the Grey Nuns took

parents, grandparents
arms reaching

the voices of five-year-olds
ten years gone

thinning into winds,
their names and braids

taken
with their clothes.

They stand shorn
and uniformed and numbered

in white smocks,
laced boots.

Over and ended
the daily rituals

taking up their sisters' hair,
combing and plaiting

their mothers'
mothers' skills

how to soften buckskin, to
brain and smoke a hide

patterns of quill
of beadwork.

Cropped out with dances,
ceremonies

ancestors whose
names they wore

like shawls, like stars, like stories.

Five unknown girls, measured
by anthropologists

arranged and photographed,
specimens in an awkward row.

Eighty years later, hanging
in a museum

relatives find them,
look into their eyes

uneasy but unbroken
whisper thanks.

When they leave, an attendant
sees five yellow post-its, sitting

in a ragged line
along the frame

on each, in Niitsitapi, a name.

THE CROW

Massif on
the horizon

looms like a
koan

holds us
in its grip.

Our eyes return;
will not give it up.

We make of our
whole being

a great inquiry.
Press close to rock.

Blink
at a huge thought

of lithic inversion:

what it takes
to displace

an entire mountain;
what it takes

the mountain
to remain, an

estranged, quiet
outlier

a weathered impenetrable
keep.

RIM

Are there horizons
where there is no horizontal

where mountains fold space,
hold distance up?

Embedded in a canyon
our heads tilt instinctively.

Here earth meets sky,
we can reach it; the rim

does not shimmer and recede.

We lean into diagonal lives,
relieved of right angles

eyes, arms, hearts drawn
upward, vectored to ridgelines

keenly aware of the slant
of time, its shape and substance;

it is a wedge; it moves
along ray-stroked slopes;

we pass into it,
are passed over.

PORTALS

Before the squalls of our
arrival, after the whimpers

that carry us away, they spin

white sentinels of some
less linear species.

Sleek, gleaming guardians
of this lonely patch,

Earth.

Tucked in the mouth
of canyons, turning.

Unhurried.   Sedated.

Horses graze below;
wild again, remote.

Blades, dip, rise, churn
aeolian waters   elegant

wands of energy, waiting
for someone – not us

beyond us – to return.

Strung on ridges, they
draw the eye after, until

sight sheers into diagonals
and they diminish,

wink out. They flank
the North Sea. Plunge

inverted anchors into chill
conflicting currents,

breathe rhythmically

great lungs of a world that is
moving on   without us.

Fish slip, flicker among them.
Seaweed tangles at their base.

Massive thwumps of air –
the pauses between them

measured, even, reassuring –

send out a steady aural pulse.

HOLDING ON

Here is an elegy for the vestigial

> wings of emu and kiwi
>> stirring when the flightless
>> remember flight.

In the semilunar fold of the human
> eye, a third eyelid
>> withers.

Something in a minor key to soothe
the remanent, a lament

> aligned like an element
>> in magnetic flux once
>>> a field has passed

> or magnetite in the beak of a
> migrating bird tugged
>> by the world below.

Music to console the residual, in
tempo *sostenuto*. Composed
in pulses. Beating hearts.

A song for what remains.

NOTES

"Sentipensante"

The term *sentipensante,* or sensing-thinking, refers to language that speaks the truth. It was invented by those who fish the Columbian Coast, according to Eduardo Galeano. As he goes on to ask: "Why does one write, if not to put one's pieces together? Education chops us into pieces; it teaches us to divorce soul from body, and mind from heart."

"Bunahan"

Nearly 90% of the 7000 or so languages that are still with us will disappear, or be disappeared, before the century ends, according to linguists. The italicized words are from Boro, an endangered language still spoken in parts of northern India. For more on this story see Mark Abley's *Spoken Here: Travels Among Threatened Languages* (Houghton Mifflin Co., 2003).

"Beads"

When Spanish monks came to Peru with the Conquistadores, they destroyed the Inca *quipos*, knotted pieces of string used to record the Quechua language phonetically, to relate history, and for enumeration. The monks thought them idolatrous. "Their loss," a Catholic Encyclopedia observes, "is by no means important, as no study, however profound, could possibly unriddle the system upon which they were based." The Inca, however, continued to use them in secret.

"The Walmart of Languages"

The last stanza of this poem is indebted to an observation by Richard Grounds (Yuchi) in *Spoken Here: Travels Among Threatened Languages* by Mark Abley.

"Tecumseh's Return: The Quakes of 1811-1812"

The words in the opening quotation were spoken by the great Shawnee chief, Tecumseh, in his efforts to create an alliance of North American tribes that might more effectively resist the incursions of the settlers and their seizure of Native lands. Although repeated in several different contexts, they are most often cited as his prophetic parting comment to the Muscogee chief, Big Warrior (in Tuckhabatchee, Alabama on 20 September 1811), who was reluctant to pledge his people to the alliance. Tecumseh then returned to Detroit, and soon a series of earthquakes began that were so powerful they caused the Mississippi River to flow backwards.

"Brinco"

The act of crossing the border from Mexico into the United States is called the "*brinco*", or "jump", in Spanish.

"Tripping"

This poem is loosely based on the interview notes of Dr. Sandra McGunigall-Smith with prisoners on Utah's death row. They describe how they cope with their near-complete isolation in Supermax units using a phenomenon they call 'tripping' which takes years to master.

"Grass"

This poem is indebted to Dr. Sandra McGunigall-Smith's research on death row inmates, especially her interview with Joe Parsons, who requested that she be a witness to his execution by the state of Utah.

"The Afterlife of Joseph Paul"

Joseph Paul Jernigan was a convicted felon executed by the State of Texas in 1993. He has since become known as "The Visible Man". As Catherine Waldby observes, Jernigan "died a new form of death. His body, annihilated in real space, was reconstituted in virtual space. The virtual corpse can be animated and programmed for interactive simulations ..."

"Something Wonderful"

This poem is for Basin, Montana and all those who continue to believe in it.

"A Vanishing"

The title of this poem is drawn from an installation of the same name by Rachel Berwick.

"Thylacine"

In 1936, the last known thylacine (also known as the "Tasmanian tiger") died – a captive in Tasmania's Hobart Zoo. In 2008, scientists "resurrected" a gene from it by implanting the gene in a mouse. Is it possible to bring back a thylacine? According to geneticist Michael Archer, "Technically I think this is pretty difficult at the moment but ... I'm personally convinced this is going to happen." According to evolutionary biologist Michael Hofreiter, "The problem with extinct animals is that they're extinct."

"Deliquescence in the Atacama"

The title of this poem, and much of its content, is drawn from an article in *Astrobiology Magazine* by Henry Bortman, July 2006.

"The Music We Cannot Hear"

"... every cluster and group of galaxies has its own note. So if you look at the whole universe, there are many tunes being played." – Andy Fabian, astronomer

"Within, Without"

The italicized lines of this poem are borrowed from Scott Abbott, a writer and professor at Utah Valley University.

"Man With Light in His Fingers"

This painting by Sky Patterson hangs in the Barn of the Robert M. MacNamara Foundation. The painting is of his uncle, Kerry Crouch, who killed himself after a long struggle with mental illness.

"Moving Hands"

The hands and fingers of those who are dying often move, restlessly – sometimes even when they do not appear to be conscious. Beyond the reference in the Hawaiian dictionary mentioned below ("String Figures"), I was unable to learn more about this. So I asked a friend of mine, Ray Weglarz, an RN who has worked at a hospice house for many years, if he had any experience with this. Here is some of what he had to say:

"What I have personally observed, many times, and have heard other hospice staff I work with say as well, is that many people in what we call, 'the actively dying process' often reach out as if to touch or feel something that is not visible to those around them. Sometimes this appears as if they were trying to pick grapes, or touch a curtain, or to touch someone or something that is unseen. Sometimes these movements/gestures do occur with a look of awe or bewilderment on the face, sometimes not. Sometimes a person will admit, not too often, that their 'mother' or another deceased relative is there with them.

"Just yesterday I heard a staff member say that during a visit with an actively dying patient she was looking at something unseen, and said to the aide, 'Do you see them?' to which the aide said, 'No' to which the patient said, 'Do you see me?' As if what she was seeing was so obvious how could she not see it, and could she see well enough to see the patient! Or, and this is just my conjecture, could the patient have felt they had crossed over somehow and perhaps they themselves were no longer visible anymore."

"String Figures"

The only written reference I have seen to the hands and figures of the dying moving occurs in an Hawaiian dictionary. The word *hei* has many meanings. It refers to "the motion of hands and fingers, especially of the dying". It also refers to string figures (like the cat's cradle). String figures are used in many cultures to pass on information. The Maori, for example, use them to pass down *matauranga Maori*, traditional knowledge.

"Song for the Miner's Canary"

The last 200 canaries were retired from British mines in 1987.

"Turtle Mountain, Moving"

In 1903 the east face of Turtle Mountain came down, spilling 82 million tonnes of limestone onto the valley floor and partially burying the town of Frank, Alberta. It spread out over three square kilometres. How to explain this extraordinary mobility? One theory is that the debris was fluidized by sound. Strong vibrations generated acoustic energy, causing dry rocks to flow like liquid.

"The Medicine Line: Geodesy"

The italicized lines are quotes from Dennis Schornack, volunteer U.S. commissioner for the International Boundary Commission.

"Five Unknown Schoolgirls at St. Mary's"

This poem is drawn from a 1925 photograph taken by Oxford anthropologist Beatrice Blackwood on the Kainai First Nation reserve in Alberta. It is also indebted to an account of the *Lost Identities* photographic exhibition presented at Head-Smashed-In Buffalo Jump Interpretive Centre in 1999.

"The Crow"

Crowsnest Mountain is in the southernmost pass through the Canadian Rockies. Like Chief Mountain in Glacier National Park, it is a klippe – a section of geologic thrust sheet that separates from the main body of the sheet, or nappe, and then undergoes erosion. Sometimes, the nappe entirely disappears, leaving the klippe as the only evidence for its existence.

ACKNOWLEDGEMENTS

I am grateful to the editors of the following publications in which these poems first appeared, sometimes in different versions:

Agenda for "Leave-taking", "Daughters" and "Tomboy"

Amoskeag for "A Vanishing"

The Antigonish Review for "Song for the Miner's Canary"

Ardor Literary Journal for "A Listening"

Argestes for "Moving Hands"

The Binnacle for "Small Talk, at Di's Country Diner"

Borderlands for "When the Mississippi Ran Backwards"

The Dalhousie Review for "The Afterlife of Joseph Paul"

Descant for "String Figures"

Evening Street Review for "Penance"

The Fiddlehead for "Prayer"

Flash: The International Short-Short Story Magazine for "Slippers"

The Fourth River for "Man With Light in His Fingers"

Front Range for "After the Train" and "Reclamation"

Janus Head for "Cairn-keeper"

Matrix for "Turtle Mountain, Moving"

The Nashwaak Review for "Brand", "The Medicine Line: Incision", "Portals", and "Re-emergence"

The New Quarterly for "*Sentipensante*" and "Within, Without"

Nimrod: The International Journal of Prose and Poetry for "Holding On"

Palo Alto Review for "Aftershocks"

Prairie Fire for "Tecumseh's Return: The Quakes of 1811-1812"

Rattle for "*Bunahan*"

RiverSedge for "Echolocation"

Saranac Review for "The Music We Cannot Hear", "Something Wonderful" and "Terminus"

The Tampa Review for "Well Without End"

Upstairs at Duroc for "Beads"

The Windsor Review for "*Brinco*" and "Rim"

2River.org for "Five Unknown Schoolgirls at St. Mary's"

and the anthologies:

Dogs Singing: A Tribute Anthology, edited by Jessie Lendennie (Salmon Poetry, Cliffs of Moher, County Clare, Ireland, 2010) for "Animal Memory"

Imagination & Place: Weather, edited by Kelly Barth (Imagination & Place Press, Lawrence, Kansas, 2012) for "Chinooked"

Open to Interpretation: Water's Edge, edited by Anastasia Faunce (St. Paul, Minnesota: Taylor & O'Neill, 2011) for "Confluence Near Puget Sound"

For grants, fellowships and residencies that assisted in the completion of *Tether*, I am indebted to the following institutions, and the individuals who make them possible: the Artists' Enclave at I-Park, the Banff Centre for the Arts, the Gushul Studios of the University of Lethbridge, Hypatia-in-the-Woods, the Montana Artists' Refuge, the Prairie Center of the Arts, the Robert M. MacNamara Foundation, the Wallace Stegner House, Utah Valley University, Brandon University and the Canada Council for the Arts.

Among the many others to whom thanks are due, I am especially grateful to Don McKay, Dionne Brand, and Karen Solie for their generous editorial advice; to Ray Weglarz and Sandy McGunigall-Smith for the work that they do and their willingness to share it with me; to Scott Abbott for time and encouragement; to Maureen Whyte of Seraphim Editions and all those associated with her, who continue to support the art of poetry; and to my friend and companion, Alan Clarke, for enduring long absences.

This book is for my parents – for all they were, for all they still are.